Family Business Matters

Dean R. Fowler, Ph.D.

with

Peg Masterson Edquist

2nd Edition

www.deanfowler.com

ISBN-13: 978-1546477136

ISBN-10: 1546477136

Introduction

Seventy-percent of all family business transitions fail. What do successful families do to beat these odds?

We carried out a research project with over 100 successful family businesses, and through our study identified twelve critical competencies for families-in-business. The twelve competencies fall into four major categories:

- **Transforming Communication**: Family Culture, Career Satisfaction, and Family Relationships
- **Enhancing Leadership**: Successor Development, Successor Competency, and Compensation Standards
- **Creating Strategies**: Business Structure, Non-Family Management and Business Strategy
- **Building Responsible Ownership**: Management Succession, Financial Planning and Tax Planning

This collection of short articles is based on the stories of the families featured in our full-length book - *Love, Power and Money: Family Business Between Generations.*

To order our full-length book go to: –
https://www.createspace.com/7139552

You may also evaluate how well your own family business is doing against these twelve success factors by completing the Legacy Roadmap Process.

For more information on The Legacy Roadmap please link to
http://www.deanfowler.com/services/assessment-tools/

Other articles, books and MP3 Audio presentations by Dean R. Fowler, Ph.D. may be found at his web-site

www.deanfowler.com

Table of Contents

Career Satisfaction

Career satisfaction should never be taken for granted as a key to making a successful family business function. Being next in line to inherit the family business does not mean the successor is a good fit for the business, or conversely, that the business is a good fit for the successor.

The case of the Mathison family illustrates how this dilemma can cause problems for the successor. John Mathison owned a manufacturing company that had developed a specialized, highly engineered mechanical device used throughout the machine tool industry. John patented his invention and developed a successful niche market for himself and his company, which generated revenues of just under $100 million a year. His son, Todd, began to work in the company as soon as he completed college. Todd was a talented electronics engineer who saw ways to expand the company's business, building on the accomplishments of his father. However, Todd did not really enjoy running the operations side of the business. Todd's entrepreneurial nature kept him focused on new business. Over dinner on a business trip, the father and son recognized and felt the respect and trust each had for the other. Todd pledged that if he were chosen to run the company, his mother and sister would share fully in the financial rewards.

Three days after their trip, John Mathison suffered a massive coronary and died. Unfortunately, the father had delayed the preparation of a new estate plan. When John died, the old plan went into effect, splitting ownership of the business three ways: To his son, to his daughter and to his wife. Although Todd and his father had agreed in principle on a plan regarding the stock and the eventual transfer of total ownership and control of the company to Todd, their plan was never legally implemented. Todd felt that he needed to take care of his mother and sister, yet he lacked the real desire to run business operations. This is a case of career satisfaction and family responsibility at odds with each other. Career satisfaction allows an individual to express his or her own interests and talents, but in family businesses, young adults are often torn between their sense of loyalty to the family, opportunity for security and income through the business, and the competing needs of their own individual interests and talents which may guide them in directions distinct from the opportunities provided in the family business. Ultimately, Todd wisely chose to bring in an outsider. He hired a search firm to find a qualified company president to run the day-to-day functions, and recruiters found a respected executive from within the industry. Todd hired this executive, who became president, while Todd became chief executive officer. "I felt like I was putting an enormous puzzle together," Todd said. "With someone to run the existing business, I could focus on the opportunities that gave me the most personal career satisfaction."

Second Generation: Blessing or Curse

One of our most memorable clients was a young man who was the oldest son of a second-generation family business owner but referred to himself as a victim of the "marshmallow effect." What's that?

This client wrote an article on the subject and allowed us to reprint it for others. He calls his family business both a blessing and a curse. He explained that although it is always there as a safety net, it can also drain the motivation a person needs to achieve their ambitions.

Now, about the marshmallow effect.

"It occurs when young heirs, like me, allow themselves to be absorbed by a sweet, comfortable, and ultimately soft option that is extremely easy to get into, but almost impossible to escape from," he said.

While this may seem a lot better than most employment options in our current economy, this client is smart to be aware of this potentially dangerous lure. The marshmallow effect can have serious consequences in most cases because someone who drifts into a career will likely never experience professional satisfaction.

He or she is also likely to suffer from a lack of self-confidence, never sure whether his position is a product of effort or name. This can lead to low morale and family conflict, because the person often blames or resents other relatives or the business for his lack of happiness.

The business suffers, too, because uninspired employees do not achieve results. Although this young family business member has no desire to join the family business, he said it always beckons.

"Several times in my youth I was tempted to drop everything and allow myself to be 'marshmallowed' -- when the money became tight, or the going got tough," he said.

The saving grace for him came in the form of a "five-year rule" imposed by the company that states no family member may enter the business without at least five years' experience elsewhere. It is designed so that family members who come into the business do so by choice, and with skills and experience that will benefit the organization. It also prevents offspring from drifting into the business without having first attempted to develop themselves and their potential.

"It forced me to motivate myself to work harder. And if I do someday enter the business, I'll know that it will be my work that will have gotten me there."

Sibling Rivalry

Sibling rivalry is a term most often associated with children; young brothers and sisters jealously struggle for their parents' attention. Rivalry may continue into adulthood, and as such it can devastate your family and undermine your business. This rivalry between siblings actively involved in a family-owned business takes two different forms: emotional and strategic. To find solutions to resolve conflicts among brothers and sisters in family businesses, one must first determine if the rivalry is emotional or strategic, or some combination of both.

The siblings in the Jones family are a typical example of emotional rivalry. The two sons were in a constant battle for approval by their entrepreneurial father. The small manufacturing business was a success, and both brothers were, in fact, technically competent. They had been given increased management responsibilities at their company through the years, and finally father named each brother to the position of general manager of separate operating divisions. These operating divisions depended upon one another for the production of parts, which were then assembled into a finished product to be shipped to the customers. Because they were in an emotional rivalry for approval from their father, the brothers competed against one another to demonstrate who was best, hoping to gain their father's blessing, rather than cooperating with one another to achieve success for the business as a whole.

Because emotion-driven sibling rivalry is rooted in problems of self-esteem, the primary solution must be built on methods that encourage the adult development and individual maturity of each of the siblings. One must recognize that the primary problem is not, in fact, between the siblings, but rather between each child and their need for recognition from his or her parent. The real problem lies between the parent and child, not between the siblings. Consequently, the solution is not working with the sibling relationship, but with the relationship between the adult-child and the parent.

Requiring employment outside the family business helps in situations where sibling rivalry is emotion-based. In our judgment, the primary value of such separation is not in gaining business acumen or exposure to alternative business techniques, although these are often side benefits. Rather, outside experience is necessary to foster adult development and requires that children mature and find a foundation for their own individual success that is independent of their parents

The second type of sibling rivalry is rooted in conflict over business styles and strategies rather than family emotions. While emotion-based rivalry is really about the child and the parent, strategy-based rivalry is really about the siblings. Frequently, such strategic conflict is driven by differences in personality concerning levels of financial risk.

The sibling conflict in the Holstrom family illustrates a strategy-based case of rivalry. An opportunity to diversify the business through an acquisition became available to John and Jim, co-owners of the business that they had inherited from their father. John, who was more entrepreneurial and aggressive, saw this as a great opportunity to grow the business and, therefore, entered into discussions to pursue the acquisition. His brother, Jim, on the other hand, enjoyed the stability that the company had recently achieved and wanted to take more time to spend with his family and to diversify his assets by investments in the stock market. Since they were 50/50 owners in this business, they had to agree on a course of action. Should they acquire a new company, or should they use the profits of their successful business to diversify into other investments?

This conflict is clearly rooted in strategy, which has a very different emotional content than the struggle of emotional rivalry. Solutions to strategic rivalry require business solutions, rather than psychological growth. The Holstrom brothers needed to develop their strategic planning, along with financial analysis, to explore alternative methods for ownership of this new business venture. Business meetings with a third party mediator is critical for finding a workable solution

While the Jones case and the Holstrom case are clear-cut—one is emotional, the other strategic—there are many situations where the emotional conflict of sibling rivalry is acted out through differences in ideas about the strategy of the business. Businesses are often defeated by competitors when siblings battle emotionally against one another using the weapons of business strategy. When sibling conflict creates tensions within your family and business environment, make sure you first define the real underlying problem: is the core of the rivalry emotional or strategic? Then take the proper course of action consistent with the real issues. If family partners in the business have each achieved their own emotional maturity, and are no longer dependent on parental approval to feel good about themselves, then strategic business alternatives and conflicts are much easier to resolve.

Mediation of Disputes

Although most members of a family business think they can work out differences among themselves, the fact is most families won't even attempt to discuss sensitive issues until it reaches a critical stage. At this point, we recommend mediation as a key strategy towards resolution.

One such family, let's call them the Angis, are a classic example of this unresolved conflict. Doug Angi ran a general contracting business for more than 20 years and had achieved a reputation as a shrewd businessman. Doug had five children, three of whom entered the business after completing college. Doug's eldest son, Jim, entered the business after earning a master's degree in finance and working at a larger accounting firm.

Although Jim was the most qualified of all the siblings to run the business, he and his father had very different opinions on key business decisions, and Jim was reluctant to work with Doug's management team on projects. As a likely successor, Jim wanted to develop his own staff and promote new people into important positions within the company.

Doug frequently stated that he was retiring; however he continued to maintain regular contact with his staff which undermined Jim's authority. Jim's two siblings who worked in the business felt torn between the wishes of their father and those of their brother, and neither wanted to make a choice as to whom they would support.

These tensions over leadership and management style are common in family businesses. Often the founding entrepreneur has developed a strong support staff that carries out his or her wishes and desires as dutiful lieutenants. This was the case with Doug, and Jim knew he wanted to replace several staff members once his father left the business. This created a tense situation that left Doug feeling his son was too stubborn to accept his management style, and Jim feeling that his father was simply not letting go of the business.

The conflict between the two generations as they struggle to share the spotlight is a symptom of their inability to clarify their own personal needs, agree on objectives, and set clear boundaries of responsibility and articulate performance expectations.

How to achieve this enlightenment? One way is through a mediation process. Mediation is a voluntary process in which the mediator guides the family business members toward their own agreement. The decisions reached by the family members are their own solutions, not those chosen by the mediator. An effective mediation process involves several key elements, including assessment, identifying underlying needs, having a family business meeting, and reaching agreement.

Although this may sound unstructured, the outcome of family business mediation must be formalized. This formalized agreement might include modification of the corporate bylaws, buy/sell agreements or job descriptions. Often, the recommendations of the outside professional consultants are not coordinated in support of the resolutions reached at the family-business meeting. The family-business consultant should work to coordinate the insurance, legal, accounting, and strategic business planning aspects as well, so that all the outside advisors are working toward the family's common agreed-upon goals.

Family Employment

Sooner or later, every business owner asks: "Should family members join the business?" Whether it's your spouse, your siblings or your children, hiring family members has both advantages and disadvantages, and it is perhaps the biggest challenge a business owner faces regarding management. To sort through the complexities of this decision, we recommend that you evaluate both sides of the issue:

Advantages:

- Improved customer relations through family contact

- Intergenerational continuity

- Long-term stability

- Shared values

- Loyalty and commitment

- Inherent trust

- Willingness to sacrifice for the business

Disadvantages:

- Possible managerial incompetence

- Lack of exposure to other businesses

- Inability to separate family and work

- Patterns of conflict rooted in early family experience

- Communication breakdowns

- Inability to retire and let go

- Nepotism

- Sibling Rivalry

Before hiring a family member, review both the pros and cons with a trusted member of senior management, a board member or a professional business counselor. Statistics tell us that 87% of all owners select a family member as the next president. If you are considering this step, make sure your successor is both competent and emotionally ready to take on the challenges of leadership.

Successor competency deals with broad-based knowledge of the business and capability as a manager. This is critically important to overcome the inherent problems of nepotism. Nepotism, as you may know, is the tendency to provide favoritism to family members and thereby undermine the growth and development of non-family managers within the family business.

Above all, potential successors must develop their own sense of personal authority and be competent in carrying out their roles and responsibilities as the future leaders of the family business. This requires that they develop a strong sense of their own self-esteem. To encourage the development of self-sufficiency, family members should establish themselves as separate and independent from the business before applying for full-time employment.

Also, clarify compensation issues for family members. Compensation levels for family members should be based on good business practices rooted in industry standards or regional area pay rates, as well as being tied to the level of performance of family members in carrying out the roles and responsibilities of the business. While the general public may feel that family members are highly compensated when they work at family businesses, research data indicates that family members are typically under-compensated. It is often assumed that this lower level for pay will be made up by the equity opportunities provided through stock ownership. In many family businesses, family compensation is not directly tied to the performance or market values, but rather, is established for reasons of family equality. Take time to consider how you will compensate family members in the business, and use those criteria as a guidepost for future employment decisions.

Your family business should consider establishing rules of entry or a more thorough family participation plan, which clarifies the requirements that family members must meet before gaining full-time employment at the company.

Performance Standards

In one of our case studies, we profile a family that has employed two sons-in-law as part of the sales staff. As the sales force grew in the company, the two, let's call them Jim and David, consistently were ranked at the bottom of the sales force, so much that their sales volume barely covered their salaries. While the President of the company, Kevin, who was their father-in-law, allowed this behavior to continue, things changed dramatically when the father met with an untimely death and his eldest son Mark took over. Mark immediately set sales criteria and challenged Jim and David to meet these objectives. Jim and David were outraged and quit the business, only asking for their jobs back the next day. Mark refused to grant their request and his sisters have not spoken to him since the incident.

To avoid this kind of problem. Successful family businesses establish adult relationships and clear performance standards to measure and evaluate family members as well as other managers within the company. In developing performance standards:

- Develop clear job descriptions that outline the responsibilities and clarify the boundaries between different jobs/roles in the company

- Set objectives to be completed by a specific date

- Create a board of advisors/directors who oversee measurements and standards for family members

- Use upward evaluation tools

By not using these tools, the business will learn a painful lesson - much like the one Kevin's company learned: A business cannot be run under two separate sets of standards – one for the family employees and one for all other employees. Ultimately, nepotism can destroy both the family and the business. This is a common problem faced by owners of family businesses. Many see this issue as a choice between the family and the company, but if you establish adult responsibility coupled with performance standards, a healthy family can operate a company using solid business criteria.

Compensating Family Members

Recently, a client called with a question about his daughter. His son had worked at the business for the past 10 years. Over the Easter holidays, his daughter had commented that she would love to come to work at the family business. As a CPA with experience at a public accounting firm, she was ready for a new challenge. With the business growing, there would be an opportunity for her, but the father's question was, "What should I pay her? Should she start at a salary comparable to the one she was making at the CPA firm? Or should her salary be equal to her brother's salary?"

One of the most challenging issues for a family business concerns compensation for family members. National studies indicate that the owners of family businesses have total compensation packages larger than those paid to non-owner presidents. Yet successor-generation family employees typically earn less total compensation at the family owned business then they would in a similar position at a business that is not owned by the family.

While the dollar amount offered to family members is critical, the more pressing issue, raised by many clients, is one of fairness. Should family members be paid equally, or should it depend on their roles and responsibilities in the company, experience, expertise and years of service? For most families, equality is considered fundamental to family life and it plays a key role in determining compensation. But it is a flawed model and can cause serious resentment from other family members as well as non-family employees.

We recommend that families consider the following three elements in designing a different compensation package for each individual in the family:

Base Pay. The base salary for any position should be consistent with salaries and wages paid for comparable positions at similarly sized businesses. Wage and salary information is available from many sources on a regional basis as well as an industry specific basis. Use this to also establish an upper and lower range for each position in the business.

Qualifications and Expertise. Does a family employee have the necessary technical and educational background to meet the job requirements? Do they have outside experience relevant to the responsibilities of their position at the family business? The family should define the qualifications and characteristics of the ideal job candidate and then measure the family member against this standard

Contribution. Positions of responsibility in any business have two aspects: day-to-day operational and long-range strategic. The owner needs to define very clear goals and objectives for measuring both types of responsibilities. Too often, family members complain that they do all the work while their siblings fail to carry their share of the load. Without measurable performance standards, families find it difficult or impossible to hold family members accountable.

Roles, responsibility, and contribution are rarely equal. While families often use equal pay to promote family harmony, these plans typically backfire; creating tensions and discord among family members and non-family members as well. Establishing a compensation plan on sound business criteria which is understood and agreed to by all of the family members and consistent with similar compensation packages for non-family employees is the best way to manage family compensation.

Strategic Planning for Family Business

Often, the mid-life transition for the older generation occurs simultaneously with the entry of children into the family business, and at the other end of the spectrum, when the children reach mid-life and the parents are retiring from the business. This period between age 40 and 50 often coincides with the maturing of the business.

For these reasons, the mid-life transition signals a critical time for the business to clarify strategic business plans in order to guarantee that the goals and objectives of the business are consistent with the needs and long-range objectives of the key family managers.

When explaining the strategic planning process to clients, we often use the analogy of a fishing expedition. To be successful as a fisherman, you need to first determine what kind of fish you hope to catch. When you know that you are fishing for, you can determine the type of equipment you will need, the type of bait required, and even the time of day to fish.

Furthermore, such a fishing expedition might require hiring a guide familiar with the territory. As a guide to family businesses working through the strategic planning process, we have identified six areas that must be evaluated:

Know your customers. Analyze your existing business and existing range of customers. Do you have an understanding of their demographics and characteristics? Are your current product and service offerings meeting their needs? As a first step, get these issues resolved through study and analysis. This can provide an excellent learning experience for family successors by helping them understand the business in greater detail.

Evaluate your strengths and weaknesses. This will fall into a broad range of categories, such as work force, equipment, technical skills, management depth and so forth. Ask key managers and employees to critically evaluate these components to more clearly define the niche market focus of your business. In addition to valuable information, this promotes goodwill among non-family employees.

Growth questions

Determine your opportunities for growth. For this, you need a detailed study of the marketplace, including both your potential customer base and opportunities among the company's competitors. At this point, there are choices to be made.

Do you want to continue offering your existing products and services to new customers? Do you want to expand the range of products and services you offer to your existing customer base? Which opportunities fit with the passions and interests of the successors? These decisions should come after a thorough survey with your existing customer base and exploration of potential customers.

Implement the plan and stay focused. In our experience, this is the most crucial step. We have worked with many closely-held businesses where the planning process takes place, yet day-to-day operations of the business are unaffected by the plan. The actual execution of the plan requires clear goals and objectives, with defined responsibilities and measurable criteria for carrying out the actions necessary to implement the plan. Family successors should be part of the implementation process with their own measurable goals and objectives tied back into the plan.

Hold regular strategic review meetings. These are to make sure that the plan is carried out and is on target. As in any business, there is a natural tendency to become focused on the day-to-day responsibilities of meeting customer demands and lose sight of implementation. We believe a family business should hold -- at minimum -- quarterly meetings to review the plan.

Define clear roles and responsibilities. By doing this, it is much easier to clarify the roles and duties of family members, and to establish accountability standards. Such standards not only guide the implementation process but also support development of family members as future leaders of the business.

Successful Habits of Successors

For the past 20 years, I have had the privilege of coaching numerous family business leaders as they have sought to balance their distinct roles as family members, managers in the business, and owners of a family legacy. Many have participated in my monthly round-table peer groups – The Forums for Family Business. What is really impressive is that these family business leaders and successors have beaten the odds of success. While nationally 70 percent of family businesses fail to transition with family ownership from one generation to the next, the 60 participants that have been in my Forums for Family Business have experienced more than a 90% success rate!

Why the high success rates? I attribute much of what they have accomplished to the seven habits of highly successful successors, a list of what they have taught me are the essential ingredients for successful families in business. The seven are: Independence, communication, competency, strategy, boundaries, liquidity strategies and the willingness to take financial risks.

The first two – establishing adult independence and re-shaping communication dynamics -- nurture healthy family relationships and typically develop during a successor's 20s. The next three -- demonstrating competency, participating in strategic decisions and clarifying boundaries -- provide the framework for management responsibilities and grow during the successor's 30s. Finally, the development of liquidity strategies and the courage to take financial risk transforms the successor's role as a passive shareholder into a proactive participant in the ownership of the business. This final stage of mastery typically occurs during the successor's late thirties and forties.

These seven habits of successful successors can't be developed all at once; they represent a gradual process, with each habit building on the previous one, over a time span of about 25 years. As family members, successors must first take the initiative to develop adult independence and re-shape family communication patterns. In their role as managers, they must develop technical competency and demonstrate leadership; they must also help to shape the business's strategic plan and must clarify the boundaries that distinguish operational, strategic and financial roles. As owners, successors must be proactive in designing liquidity strategies and then be willing to assume financial risk to consolidate ownership for their generation.

A cornerstone to this process is patience, which is mastered when successors exhibit the first habit -- adult independence – successfully. This is the foundation for the successful implementation of the other six habits, and will ensure a successful transition. Coaches and mentors must teach successors the virtue of patience by embodying this virtue themselves. Mastery of the seven habits of highly successful successors is a challenging process that requires not only the proactive involvement of the successor, but also the willingness of the senior generation and other family members to accept and encourage the transition from generation to generation.

Board of Directors

By its nature, family owned businesses are ruled and governed by members of the same family, yet should the family have complete control over the company? One owner of a local manufacturing firm, which has had an outside board of directors for 30 years, said outside boards are a necessity. "It's not only wise to have an outside board from a corporate governance standpoint, but it's also wise as a practical matter to seek the professional guidance of others so you don't get trapped in tunnel vision when guiding your company."

Nationally, fewer than ten percent of family businesses have outside (non-family, non-management) board members. Yet, outside boards are extremely effective in providing expertise for the management issues faced by family-owned businesses. Because they face unique issues, three distinct vehicles should serve the needs of the family business:

A Legal Board of Directors to address ownership issues made up of persons representing different ownership interests

A Family Council to provide a place for family members, both active and non-active, to keep informed about the business and to resolve issues rooted in family dynamics

An Outside Advisory Board to draw upon the expertise and experience of other business owners and presidents on topics related to strategic and operational business and management issues

Many times your legal board can function as your advisory board as well, but make sure you understand the dynamics of the relationship. First, the CEO/president needs to make a personal commitment to accept the advice and be accountable to the board. Second, outside boards are most successful when the membership is made of experienced and qualified board members. Third, expectations need to be clearly stated so that board members understand their roles and responsibilities. Fourth, the length of service should be clearly stated and staggered terms should be defined so that board members do not retire at the same time.

Fairness in Family Business

A recent client came to me with a common problem among family business owners who are in the early stages of succession planning. This problem routinely occurs when there are only one or two children active in the business, and yet the parents want to have all of their children benefit from their good fortune.

The Millstone family is a perfect example of this dilemma. Calvin and Mary Millstone owned a second-generation manufacturing business started by Mary's father. Two of their six children, Charlie and Cynthia, were active in the business. By the time Calvin reached his 61st birthday, all of the non-voting stock of the company had been equally gifted to his six children. This represented 90 percent of the equity of the corporation.

The couple then agreed to sell their voting control interests to their son and daughter. This arrangement seemed fair to the parents, but not to their active children. While Cynthia and Charlie had 100 percent of the voting control, they each owned only 20 percent of the total equity of the corporation. The working siblings wanted not only total control of the business, but total ownership as well.

From the senior generation's perspective, it is quite common to understand the family business as an asset to benefit all family members, independent of their management roles and responsibilities in the company. The family business is a legacy created by the senior generation, and now gifted graciously to their descendants.

However, from the employed successor generation's perspective, the question of "fairness" often takes a different twist. Most successors employed in key management positions in the company believe that future profits and the increase in the equity of the corporation are a direct result of their own sweat equity -- of their personal contribution and effort to the success of the business. Accordingly, they believe this growth should benefit their own personal estates -- not the estates of their inactive siblings.

While many managing successors recognize a responsibility to provide adequate financial resources to their parents for the rest of their lifetime, very few have a similar sense of responsibility and obligation to their inactive siblings.

In most entrepreneurial family businesses, a single shareholder has been both the owner and the manager of the business. In second and future generations, it is quite common for multiple shareholders to own the business, and for a limited number of shareholders to be active in the management of the business. Family-owned businesses, therefore, must make distinctions between the benefits of ownership and the responsibilities of management. There are two basic alternatives that families-in-business should explore to resolve these long-term issues concerning power and money:

- Create a "quasi-public" corporation that separates ownership from management.

- Create a method for family members actively employed in the company to buy out their inactive siblings.

Calvin Millstone understood the concerns of Cynthia and Charlie, and designed a family business plan providing a stock redemption plan so they could eventually purchase the non-voting shares of the inactive siblings.

Transferring a Family Business

One family owner faced a dilemma recently: How could he transfer the business to the next generation, protect his future financial needs, but treat each of his children equally, and still make sure the business could operate successfully? This dilemma is common to most owners of family businesses, especially when tax savings are the primary forces driving estate-planning decisions.

Clearly, developing an effective estate plan is a complex procedure and requires the owners of family businesses to make very tough choices. Perhaps this is the reason that only half of all family businesses have estate plans in place. Given the fact that the federal estate tax rates are as high as fifty-five percent, failure to plan for the future has tremendous financial consequences.

What are the tough choices? Based on our work resolving conflicts caused by estate planning decisions, four key questions must be asked and then resolved:

Question 1: Do you have a competent successor who is qualified to provide strong leadership for the business?

Question Two: Should your surviving spouse have voting control of the corporation?

Question Three: Should voting control be shared equally by all your children?

Question Four: Who should benefit from the financial success of the business?

Once you've answered those questions, you can begin the process of creating an estate plan. In addition, consider the direction the successor will take in terms of future decisions about wealth distribution. Conflict usually arises because the successors actively employed in the business are assuming that they will be the future entrepreneurs, yet the parents and inactive siblings are assuming that the designated successors will work for the broad-based benefit of the entire family.

- To avoid conflict around the issues of wealth, family businesses should consider some of the following options:

- If possible, divide your estate so that the operating company is owned only by those actively employed in the business

- Clearly distinguish between management and ownership income

- Establish liquidity agreements in the buy-sell agreement. That is, have provisions that give minority share-holders the right to sell their stock

- Use insurance or other methods to buy-out minority shareholders.

The Authors

Dean R. Fowler, Ph.D.

Dean R. Fowler, Ph.D. is recognized as one of the world's leading experts specializing in the emotional dynamics that impact families in business and families of wealth. The international association, The Family Firm Institute, honored him by selecting him to receive the prestigious "Award for Interdisciplinary Achievement". His book – Love, Power and Money – has won world-wide acclaim in reviews in the major publications dealing with family enterprises as one of the best books on integrated family transition planning.

In 2008 he was appointed to serve with a select group of business leaders on the Coleman Chair Advisory Council at Marquette University's College of Business Administration.

In 2009 a new television series – Family Inc. – was launched in five Midwestern states with Dean Fowler serving as host. (family-inc.com)

In 2011 he published two additional books – Family Business Success Factors and Proactive Family Business Successors. Both books are available as MP3 downloads at his web-site: http://www.deanfowler.com/resources/books-cds/

For over thirty years, Dean Fowler has served over 300 family clients in both the United States and Europe. His firm, Dean Fowler Associates, provides integrated services focusing on the "soft side of hard issues" by working closely with the other professional advisors trusted by the family client. For more information, see www.deanfowler.com

Peg Masterson Edquist

Peg Masterson Edquist is a freelance journalist with more than thirty five years of broadcast journalism and print journalism experience. During her career, she has worked for the *Milwaukee Journal/Sentinel* as a business writer, covering beats as varied as retailing and the brewing industry. For 20 years she was a contributing writer, broadcast reporter and columnist with the *Business Journal of Greater Milwaukee.*

During her freelance career, she has written for publications that include *Advertising Age, The Writer* and *Photo District News*. She is co-author of the book "The Transport of Hope, *How one humanitarian made a difference in the Balkan conflict*" (HenschelHAUSbooks June 2016 $14.95) She and her husband Jerry, are owners of Carlson Tool & Manufacturing, Inc., a $27 million Wisconsin manufacturing firm with 150 employees. Carlson Tool is a privately held, family-owned business founded by Jerry's father in 1958

Confidentiality Statement

Since 1983 I have been privileged to work with over 300 family-owned businesses. The owners and families of these businesses have taught me about the challenges they face, and have demonstrated both the measures of success and the root causes of failure facing their businesses as they have lived through the transition between generations.

Confidentiality is critically important to all families in business. Therefore, all of the stories used throughout this book are composite hypotheticals, drawing on specific situations I have encountered but never identifying the families involved. The stories illustrate the issues that face most family businesses in one way or another, but none of the stories represent a real situation. All have been disguised by combining common trends from several cases, inventing the names of family members and changing the names and locations of the businesses and other related characteristics. These changes have been made to make the real sources unrecognizable. Given these changes, any similarity to a real family business case is purely coincidental, unintended and unknown to me.

www.ingramcontent.com/pod-product-compliance
Lightning Source LLC
Chambersburg PA
CBHW061240180526
45170CB00003B/1376